GUILTY, GUILTY, GUILTY!

In this **Doonesbury** volume, Marvelous Mark Slackmeyer's endearing ravings go entirely unabridged. His WBBY Watergate broadcasts, which caused such consternation among the nation's newspaper editors, herein are happily published along with Pat Nixon's testimony to the Ervin Committee, Ron Zeigler's alleged press briefings, Superstar Jeb Magruder's smash lecture tour, and inevitably, R. M. "Dick" Nixon's Operation Candor. And for those who have wearied of wallowing, GUILTY, GUILTY, GUILTY! has other surprises: Yuri Yetsky, Russian man of letters; Skip Willis, POW in a time-warp; and Zonker Harris, mail-person and screener of bad tidings.

THE DOONESBURY PHENOMENON

In less than five years, a remarkable new comic strip called **Doonesbury** has provoked more public and media reaction than any cartoon in the last twenty years, winning legions of loyal followers and becoming the first comic strip awarded the Pulitzer Prize. Michael J. Doonesbury and the denizens of Walden commune appear in nearly four hundred newspapers with a readership of over 23 million.

D1207751

Bantam Books by G. B. Trudeau

CALL ME WHEN YOU FIND AMERICA
GUILTY, GUILTY, GUILTY!

Guilty, Guilty, Guilty!

A Doonesbury Book • by G. B. Trudeau

BANTAM BOOKS
TORONTO NEW YORK LONDON

To Annie, of course

GUILTY, GUILTY, GUILTY!

A Bantam Book / published by arrangement with
Holt, Rinehart and Winston

PRINTING HISTORY

Holt, Rinehart and Winston edition / June 1974
2nd printing......August 1974   3rd printing......April 1975

Bantam edition / March 1976

Published simultaneously in the United States and Canada

Bantam Books are published by Bantam Books, Inc. Its trade-
mark, consisting of the words "Bantam Books" and the por-
trayal of a bantam, is registered in the United States Patent
Office and in other countries. Marca Registrada. Bantam
Books, Inc., 666 Fifth Avenue, New York, New York 10019.

PRINTED IN THE UNITED STATES OF AMERICA

0 9 8 7 6 5 4 3 2 1

1

ARE THERE ANY MORE QUESTIONS?

MR. YETSKY, IS IT TRUE YOU WERE ONCE SELF-EFFACING?

DA. I CONFESS THAT WHEN I CAME TO THIS COUNTRY YEARS AGO, MY SPIRIT WAS LACKING IN CONFIDENCE. BUT ONE FALL DAY, AS I DROVE THROUGH MICHIGAN TO A READING IN DETROIT, I WAS BLESSED WITH A VISION!

MY GENIUS CAME TO ME IN A REVELATION! "YETSKY," I SAID, "IT'S TRUE, COMRADE—YOU ARE INDEED THE EXTRAORDINARY MORTAL! YOU ARE... TRUTH!"

WHEN I REACHED DETROIT, I BOUGHT MY SHADES.

YOUNG MAN, I WOULD APPRECIATE MY SPEAKER'S FEE BEFORE I LEAVE. MY EXPENSES, UNHAPPILY, HAVE BEEN HIGH.

WHAT? ARE YOU NOT PAID WELL AT HOME?

NO. I ENJOY NO SPECIAL LUXURY. YOU SEE, I AM A POET AND SOCIALIST. ALL MY "POSSESSIONS" ARE SPIRITUAL.

THAT CERTAINLY WASN'T THE IMPRESSION WE GOT WHEN YOU DROVE UP TO THE HALL THIS MORNING.

A TACTLESS REFERENCE TO MY FERRARI, I ASSUME?

WELL... YEAH.

Thesis proposal.

TAP
TAP

In my paper, I intend to outline the major positive aspects of our involvement in Vietnam.

TAP
TAP

I will take as comprehensive an approach as possible, but it should be noted there are many problems in writing such a thesis.

TAP
TAP

Ridicule and abuse from my friends, to name two.

TAP
TAP

MY FELLOW ALUMNI, THE FINANCIAL SITUATION AT THE UNIVERSITY IS GRAVE. WE MUST HAVE YOUR SUPPORT IF WE ARE TO MAINTAIN OUR STANDARDS OF EXCELLENCE.

SO, LADIES AND GENTLEMEN, I OPEN UP THE FLOOR TO YOUR PLEDGES. HOW MUCH DO I HEAR FOR THE FUTURE OF HIGHER EDUCATION IN AMERICA?!

GOING ONCE, GOING TWICE...

HEY! A LETTER FROM PHRED! IT'S ABOUT TIME!

"DEAR RUNNING DOG: PLEASE FORGIVE MY DELINQUENCY IN NOT WRITING YOU SOONER. I HAVE BEEN TRÉS BUSY."

"RIGHT AFTER THE CEASE-FIRE, I SHED MY WICKED WAYS AND OPENED UP THE DELTA'S FIRST SOUVENIR SHOP."

NO!

NINE BUCKS?!

LOOK, MAN, I GOT A FAMILY TO FEED!

POSTCARDS $1.00

Mekong Delta

Hats

WHAT IS IT, JOHN?

MR. PRESIDENT, MR. DUC THO IS ON THE PHONE FOR YOU, SIR..

HELLO, LE?.. WHAT CAN I DO FOR YOU?...YES, I'M SORRY ABOUT THE AID, BUT CONGRESS HAS TO ACT ON THAT.. NO, WE HAVEN'T GONE BACK ON OUR PLEDGE... YES, I KNOW ABOUT YOUR SCHOOLS AND HOSPITALS...BUT..

..BUT..

LOOK, DUC THO, I NEVER PROMISED YOU A ROSE GARDEN!

HEE HEE, HEE!

HA, HA, HA! VERY GOOD, SIR!

WELL, I GUESS IT'S ABOUT TIME I GOT THIS OVER WITH. I'VE PUT IT OFF TOO LONG AS IT IS..

HELLO?.. OH, HI, HONEY! IT'S MOMMY. HOW ARE YOU? TERRIFIC!.. WHAT?.. AN "A" IN READING?.. THAT'S GREAT... AND A "B+" IN SPELLING! IMAGINE!

THE ZOO?.. REALLY, WAS THAT FUN?.. YES, THE MONKEYS ARE MY FAVORITES, TOO... YES, AND THE ZEBRAS... SAY, HONEY, IS DADDY HOME?.. FINE.. YES, I'LL HANG ON..

CLINT? HI, I WANT A DIVORCE.

HEY, WHERE'S OL' MARCUS TODAY? I THOUGHT HE WAS COMING OUT FOR AN AFTERNOON DIP!

NOPE. HE HAD TO GO BARTEND TODAY AT THE REUNIONS.

BARTEND?

YEAH. HE WANTED TO WORK FOR ONE OF THE MORE RECENT CLASSES, BUT HE GOT STUCK WITH THE CLASS OF '43.

OH, NO!

AND DON'T GET ANY HAIR IN MY COCKTAIL, KID!

YESSIR.

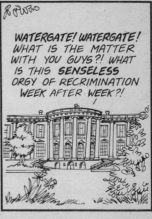

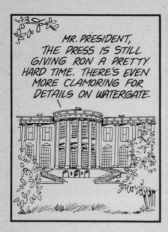

NICHOLE, HAVE YOU HEARD ABOUT MARK'S NEW SERIES OF PROFILES ON HIS RADIO SHOW?

NO. WHAT'S IT ON?

THE WATERGATE CONSPIRATORS. HE'S WORKED OUT COMPLETE BIOGRAPHIES ON ALL OF THEM.

BOY, I'LL BET THEY'RE JUST **BRUTAL!**

NOT AT ALL. I READ THEM LAST NIGHT. SOME OF THEM ARE QUITE SENSITIVE.

"LOS ANGELES IS A LONELY TOWN TO GROW UP IN, ESPECIALLY IF YOU'RE A SMALL BOY NAMED H. R. HALDEMAN."

GOOD NEWS, KIDDIES! TIME FOR ANOTHER EXCLUSIVE WBBY "*WATERGATE PROFILE*"! TODAY'S OBITUARY— *JOHN MITCHELL*!

JOHN MITCHELL, THE FORMER U.S. ATTORNEY-GENERAL, HAS IN RECENT WEEKS BEEN REPEATEDLY LINKED WITH BOTH THE WATERGATE CAPER AND ITS COVER-UP.

IT WOULD BE A DISSERVICE TO MR. MITCHELL AND HIS CHARACTER TO PREJUDGE THE MAN, BUT EVERYTHING KNOWN TO DATE COULD LEAD ONE TO CONCLUDE HE'S GUILTY!

THAT'S *GUILTY!*- GUILTY, GUILTY, GUILTY!!

HOLY MOLY, CAMPERS! TIME FOR ANOTHER WBBY "WATERGATE PROFILE"! TODAY'S COVER-UP CUTIE IS... JOHN EHRLICHMAN!

"JOHN EHRLICHMAN, THE PRESIDENT'S ADVISOR ON DOMESTIC AFFAIRS, HAS FOR FOUR YEARS BEEN A CONSIDERABLE POWER IN THE WHITE HOUSE. YET UNTIL RECENTLY, MANY AMERICANS WERE UNAWARE OF THE SCOPE OF HIS DUTIES!"

"ON THE AVERAGE DAY JOHN EHRLICHMAN USED TO CONSULT WITH MR. NIXON AT LEAST ONCE OR TWICE. IF THE WORD CAME DOWN HE WAS NEEDED, HE'D MAKE HIS WAY UP TO THE OVAL OFFICE WHERE HE WOULD INVARIABLY ENCOUNTER FELLOW STAFFER H.R. HALDEMAN!"

HALT! STOP OR I'LL SHOOT!

BOB! IT'S ME! IT'S ME!

HEEWACK! UN AUTRE "PROFILE" REQUEST! I'VE GOTTA HAND IT TO YOU, BOYS AND GIRLS — THERE'S BEEN TERRIFIC WATERGATE RESPONSE!

KEEP 'EM COMING, CAMPERS! GET THE FULL STORY — TRUTHS, INNUENDO, HEARSAY, THE WHOLE BIT — ON EVERYONE LINKED WITH THE NATION'S DARKEST SCANDAL!

FROM THE CUBAN BURGLARS TO THE CHIEF EXECUTIVE HIMSELF, IF YOU'VE GOT A FAVORITE WATERGATE CONSPIRATOR — AND YOU WANT TO KNOW MORE ABOUT HIM — REMEMBER TO PHONE IN YOUR REQUEST TO WBBY! THAT'S WBBY!!

OKAY! PROFILE OF JOHN DEAN III GOING OUT TO JOEY WITH HUGS FROM DONNA!

G.B.Trudeau

WELL, MOTHER O' MINE, IT'S TIME I LEFT FOR LAOS. I JUST GOT MY MARCHING ORDERS FROM THE PATHET LAO.

NOW YOU BE SURE TO WRITE ME IN... **HEY!** WHAT'S THIS?

IT'S A GOING-AWAY PRESENT! MOM, WHAT A **THOUGHTFUL** THING TO DO! HONESTLY...

"THE ALL-NEW **TOMMY TOURIST** GUIDE TO LAOS—1961." IT WAS ON SALE!

"UPON YOUR EXIT FROM THE **HO CHI MINH** TRAIL, TURN LEFT ONTO THE SCENIC MOUNTAIN PATH WHICH TRAVERSES THE HIGH COUNTRYSIDE."

"IF THE FERRY OVER THE MEANDERING **MEKONG** ISN'T WORKING, YOU MAY HAVE TO GET YOUR FEET WET. BE SURE TO BRING ALONG SOME DRY, LIGHTWEIGHT SUMMER CLOTHES FOR WHEN YOU REACH THE OTHER SIDE."

"A QUICK SCRAMBLE UP THE BEAUTIFUL **DINO-LINO** CLIFF FORMATION AND YOU SHOULD BE ABLE TO SPOT A SMALL LEDGE 80 YARDS ABOVE YOU. A SHORT, SPIRITED HIKE, AND THE TOURIST WILL SOON FIND HIMSELF AT THE TOP."

"WELCOME TO LAOS."

©B.Trudeau

SIR?.. OH, SIR?..

PARDON US, SIR! WE ARE DESTITUTE, HUNGRY REFUGEES ON OUR WAY TO VIENTIANE! TAKE **PITY** ON US!

WE HAVE NOT EATEN IN **DAYS**! COULD NOT SOME OF US SHARE IN THE HOT RICE DINNER YOU HAVE PREPARED FOR YOURSELF?

UM...SURE. HOW MANY ARE THERE OF YOU?

135,000.

G.B.Trudeau

AW, C'MON, LOO! CAN'T YOU EVEN FIX ME A LIGHT SNACK?

LOOK! I TOLD YOU! I'M **CLOSED**! I'VE BEEN BOMBED OUT OF BUSINESS!

LISTEN TO THIS, LOO: "WHILE THE LAOTIANS ARE A PROUD AND FIERCELY TENACIOUS PEOPLE, THEIR MOST OUTSTANDING CHARACTERISTIC IS **GENEROSITY**!

"WHETHER FOR A FRIEND IN NEED OR A PASSING STRANGER, THE LAOTIANS ARE ALWAYS QUICK ON THE DRAW WHEN IT COMES TO **KINDNESS, COMPASSION**, AND LENDING A **HELPING HAND**!

"FURTHERMORE..."

ALRIGHT ALREADY! I'LL TURN ON THE GRILL!

WELL, HENRY?..

MR. PRESIDENT, I REALIZE THE SITUATION **IS** DETERIORATING OVER THERE, BUT I'M AFRAID ABSOLUTELY **NO ONE** ACCEPTS "PROTECTIVE REACTION" AS A CREDIBLE CONCEPT THESE DAYS.

HMM... WELL, WHAT ABOUT MY OTHER IDEA?

SIR?

"CAMBODIAZATION."

FORGET IT.

GBTrudeau

DAVID, YOUR RECENT BOOK, "THE BEST AND THE BRIGHTEST" HAS REALLY TAKEN OFF! HOW DO YOU EXPLAIN IT?

I THINK, MERV, THAT THE QUESTIONS OF THE VIETNAM QUAGMIRE HAVE LED MANY PEOPLE TO BECOME CURIOUS ABOUT THESE BRILLIANT JOHNSON AND KENNEDY AIDES WHO FIRST GOT US INVOLVED OVER THERE.

WELL, I WOULD THINK THAT WOULD BODE WELL FOR YOUR NEXT BOOK, DAVID. AS I UNDERSTAND IT, RECENT EVENTS HAVE INSPIRED YOU TO START WORK ON A HOT NEW SEQUEL!

THAT'S RIGHT, MERV. IT'S CALLED "THE WORST AND THE STUPIDEST."

OH? WHAT'S IT ABOUT?

ONE FURTHER QUESTION, MR. COLSON...

WE HAVE HEARD PREVIOUS TESTIMONY TO THE EFFECT THAT YOU PROPOSED A BURGLARY AND FIRE-BOMBING OF THE BROOKINGS INSTITUTE IN 1971. WHAT SAY YOU?

OH NOW, SENATOR, THAT REMARK WASN'T MEANT TO BE TAKEN AS **SERIOUS**.. HEE-HEE.., OF COURSE NOT!... HOW RIDICULOUS!.. HOW **ABSURD!**

I WAS JUST BEING SILLY, SENATOR..

I'LL SAY.

WE INTERRUPT THE SENATE WATERGATE HEARINGS TO BRING YOU THIS SPECIAL BULLETIN.

TODAY ON THE PRE-EMPTED SOAP OPERA, "AS THE HOSPITAL TURNS," DR. HARDIN FINALLY DECIDED TO DIVORCE HIS WIFE RACHEL, AFTER FIVE YEARS OF MARRIAGE! A BITTER CUSTODY FIGHT IS EXPECTED.

TO REPEAT: DR. HARDIN IS GETTING A DIVORCE FROM RACHEL! THAT'S A FINAL.

WE NOW RETURN TO OUR REGULARLY SCHEDULED BROADCAST.

GOOD AFTERNOON. WELL, WE'VE BEEN CONFERRING LIKE CRAZY, AND I THINK WE HAVE GOT OURSELVES ANOTHER SNAPPY 5-4 DECISION.

THE SUPREME COURT OF THE UNITED STATES OF AMERICA HAS REVIEWED THE PRINCIPLE OF EXECUTIVE PRIVILEGE AS IT PERTAINS TO THE FIRST LADY. THE CONSENSUS IS THAT IT DOES NOT APPLY.

THE COURT THUS DIRECTS MRS. NIXON TO MAKE A SENATE HEARINGS APPEARANCE, INASMUCH AS IT FEELS SHE SHOULDN'T ENJOY THE IMMUNITY TO WHICH PRESIDENTIAL AIDES ARE CURRENTLY ENTITLED.

ALSO, THE COURT RATHER THINKS IT WOULD BE A GIGGLE.

GBTrudeau

YES, WHAT IS IT, MEL?

SIR, WE'VE BEEN GETTING A LOT MORE HEAT FROM CONGRESS OVER THE TAPES. PERHAPS WE SHOULD RECONSIDER..

GO AWAY, MEL. I'M MINDING THE PEOPLE'S BUSINESS.

BUT, SIR, EVEN THE LOYALIST SENATORS ARE NOW INSISTING THE PEOPLE HAVE THE RIGHT TO KNOW.

THE SENATORS ARE NOT IN A POSITION TO INSIST.

AND THE PEOPLE?

THEY SHOULD MIND THEIR OWN BUSINESS.

GOOD EVENING. WELCOME TO *ABC NEWS!*

HARRY'S ON VACATION, AND HOWARD'S ON ASSIGNMENT. FRANK IS ON THE ROAD.

SAM IS OFF THE AIR, TOM IS IN TRANSIT, AND TINA IS OUT TO LUNCH. I'M THE ONLY ONE LEFT HERE. MY NAME IS CARLOS; I WORK UPSTAIRS IN THE STOCK-ROOM.

HERE ARE TONIGHT'S HEADLINES..

SCOTTY, HOW DID YOU EVER GET SUCH **GREAT** SEATS FOR JEB MAGRUDER'S CONCERT?

IT WASN'T EASY, JOANIE!

YOU KNOW, JEB'S MY **FAVORITE** CONSPIRATOR! I DON'T KNOW WHY — MAYBE IT'S HIS BOYISH GOOD LOOKS!

WHAT'S ON THE PROGRAM FOR TONIGHT?

LEMME SEE.. THE FIRST ACT IS EXCERPTS FROM HIS DIARY. AFTER THAT THERE'S A COVER-UP SYNOPSIS, FOLLOWED BY A QUESTION-AND-ANSWER PERIOD.

THE LAST ACT IS HIS PLEA FOR FORGIVENESS AND UNDER-STANDING.

OH, I HEAR THAT'S GREAT!

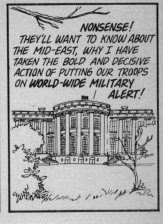

TODAY AT A PRESS CONFERENCE, THE PRESIDENT LASHED OUT AT THE TELEVISION MEDIA FOR WHAT HE CALLED BIASED COVERAGE OF THE WATERGATE AFFAIR.

SAID MR. NIXON, "IN ALL MY YEARS OF POLITICS, NEVER HAVE I SEEN SUCH OUTRAGEOUS, VICIOUS, DISTORTED, AND ERRONEOUS REPORTING!"

HE WENT ON TO CONDEMN TELEVISION COMMENTATORS FOR "THE VINDICTIVE LEERS AND SNEERS DIRECTED AT THE GREAT OFFICE OF THE PRESIDENCY."

MOST REPORTERS PRESENT AGREED THE PRESIDENT WAS BEING HIS USUAL, ASININE SELF.